How to Forgive Yourself

A Step by Step Guide to Forgiving Yourself and Letting Go of the Past

by Alona Bishop

Table of Contents

Introduction

As we move through life, it is inevitable that we will make mistakes. Sometimes, these mistakes end up hurting other people. Perhaps we have cheated on a spouse, betrayed a friend, or caused an accident. Maybe we mistreated our children, took advantage of a colleague, or took our family members for granted. We have all done things that we regret. When we have regrets, we may deal with feelings of guilt, anger, or sadness. These feelings, and the experience of regret in general, are not necessarily bad. In fact, they are evidence that we have a moral code or a sense of ethics that is important to us. It would be unnatural to never feel regret; lack of regret and guilt is a psychopathic character trait. Feeling guilt is a completely normal and healthy reaction to mistakes. Rather, it is our response to regret that often causes problems. We must learn to respond to feelings of guilt and regret in more appropriate ways.

Most of us deal with guilt in a self-criticizing manner. We often look back at past events and think, "I wish I had done things differently." These kinds of thoughts are not only painful, they are unproductive. We will never be able to go back in time to change what we have done. The past is the past; we do not have any control over it. We need to let go of these thoughts. We may also equate our actions to our identity. We

1

think that since we have done something bad, we are bad as human beings. Again, these thoughts are both incorrect and unhelpful.

Guilt left unchecked is incredibly harmful. When not acted upon in a productive way, it can cause problems with our physical and mental health. Ongoing, intense feelings of guilt are a major source of chronic stress. Chronic stress can result in anxiety disorders, trouble sleeping, depression, heart disease, digestive issues, and a weakened immune system. Guilt changes the way we view ourselves, and this shift in self-image can have negative effects on our personal and business relationships. Harboring feelings of guilt and regret is detrimental to every aspect of our lives.

There are healthier ways of dealing with past mistakes. Instead of holding on to guilt and regret, we need to use these feeling to propel ourselves forward in life. By learning to forgive ourselves, we can break free from the past and begin creating a better future for ourselves.

3

4

Chapter 1: The Real Source of Bad Feelings

The first step toward learning to forgive yourself is to identify the real cause of your nagging guilt. When we experience bad feelings associated with past mistakes, we tend to believe that our feelings are caused by the event. We think that, since we cannot go back and change what we did, we will never be able to escape our feelings of guilt, shame, anger, and sadness. However, our bad feelings are not really caused by the "bad" thing we did in the past. That event is in the past, and it has no real power or influence over us.

In truth, our bad feelings are caused by how we reacted to the event and our dissatisfaction with how we dealt with the situation. Bad feelings stem from a (mis)understanding that we did not act correctly then, and there is nothing to do about it in the present. They stem from a belief that we messed up irreparably. We are dwelling on thoughts of the "wrong" thing that we did.

The first step in forgiving yourself is acknowledging that these feelings have a tight grip on you, and it does not have to be that way, and that to keep thinking these thoughts is a voluntary *choice* you are making. If you are unconvinced, think about it this way. Consider your daily life and think about your daily routine. Think about what you do and how you feel as you move through your days and weeks. Are your feelings of guilt constant throughout your day-to-day activities and interactions? No, of course they aren't. That is because when you are busy with daily tasks, you are too busy to spend time and energy thinking about your regret over past events. Therefore, your experience of bad feelings associated with past events is actually caused by your tendency to dwell on those events in the present.

If you can acknowledge that you have the choice of whether or not to think these thoughts, you will have completed a critical first step. When confronted with any problem, the first step is to acknowledge its presence and move forward from there.

There is also the chance that you are overpowered by your guilt. Although you may be moving through your regular routine, the mind still seems preoccupied with your problem. In that case, below are some helpful exercises to attempt. They will help you break down what exactly is on your mind, and make you aware of the patterns your mind follows that leave you plagued with guilt. If you can identify exactly how your thoughts are being reproduced over and over again, you have a much stronger chance of intervening in your own thought processes and breaking the vicious cycle of guilt.

Exercises

The familiar saying, sometimes still attributed to Albert Einstein, states that *"Insanity is doing the same thing over and over again and expecting different results."* Certain exercises can make the process of forgiving yourself more deliberate so you do not fall into this trap of pursuing the same solutions over and over again.

- **Keep a journal** of the thoughts in your mind that relate to exactly what you want to forgive yourself for. By getting it down on paper, you are able to physically disconnect from the voice in your head, because the voice's words will be written on the paper. If you feel stuck, or feel that you are not accurately or satisfyingly able to write about your feelings, try a **free write**. This method involves writing non-stop for a minute, five minutes, or more. Even if you cannot think of what to write, you have to write. Even if it just says, "I don't know what to write this is hard and I don't want to go on...." A minute of writing is longer than you think and without knowing it the words turn productive at some point. This method of **writing therapy** allows you to step away from your guilt, anger, or sadness, even if only for a while, giving you time to more objectively process what is happening.

- Try to **catch yourself thinking.** There is a good chance that you have one story or a particular scene replaying over and over in your mind. It has snowballed over time, simplifying into a precise tale in which you know exactly where to place the blame -- *on yourself.* It has become so real in your head and now you cannot escape it. Integrate this habit into your daily routine for a few days: whenever you start thinking about where things went wrong, stop yourself and ask, "How did I get here?" Step out of your thoughts and figure out the stream of consciousness that got you to where you are. Log it down in your journal then go about your day. If you find yourself getting distracted with your thoughts again, stop and listen once more. Trace the thought pattern and note it. You should start to notice a connection in your thought patterns. Just as there's often a trigger that has cigarette smokers reaching for a cigarette, there are certain reasons you are arriving at some thoughts over and over again. By recognizing how you got there, you can break the link and keep yourself from getting pulled into a guilt wormhole.

- **Engage in physical activity**. If you feel as though you cannot get thoughts out of your head, try moving. If you don't have a weekly exercise routine yet, start one. Doing exercise, playing sports, dancing, or any other physical activity is a great way to distract yourself from your thoughts, and get endorphins to meet your guilt or stress with happiness.

Chapter 2: Extinguishing Negative Thoughts

If we want to forgive ourselves and move on in life, we must learn to change our thought patterns. If we can change our thought patterns, then we can avoid dwelling on past events that bring about regretful or guilty feelings. In order to change our thought patterns, we need to neutralize negative thoughts.

When we are unable to forgive ourselves, it is because we hold onto negative thoughts associated with a certain event. We must look at the event from a different perspective. For example, when we feel guilty for something, it is because we think that our action created a bad outcome. However, this point of view is extremely limited. The simple fact is we do not know all of the effects or entire outcome of our actions. Is it possible that something good was made possible by what you perceive to be a negative outcome?

Let's say that you caused an accident that put a man in the hospital. This, you assume, is a bad outcome. But is it possible that, while in the hospital, this man met a nurse who turned out to be the love of his life? Or is it possible that, during some routine scans at the

13

hospital, a potentially fatal disease was caught early and the man's life was saved? When working toward forgiving yourself, it is helpful to adopt the point of view that **everything happens for a reason**. From this perspective, it is possible that the "bad" outcome that your actions caused was actually just a necessary stepping stone toward something great.

But what if you cannot find the silver lining? What to do then? **Relax your internal sense of agency** that is leading you to feel guilt. This is especially important if you are feeling guilty about something that was not directly caused by you. It is important to recognize that all circumstances are a mixture of nature's and human actions. Think here of the butterfly effect, where seemingly inconsequential factors lead to potentially large circumstances. What this means is that it is really difficult to identify the exact causes of any particular situation—you only have a part of the story. What you are doing is in effect taking this part of the story that you have and telling yourself it is the reality. By recognizing that your negative thoughts are limited and subjective, you are able to replace these thoughts with more productive ones.

Another way we can shift perspectives is by realizing that **we are all products of our environment**. When we do something "bad", we automatically assume that we are to blame for the outcome associated with the "bad" thing that we did. However, consider this: are you always in control of your actions? I would venture to say that no one is in control of their actions one hundred percent of the time. That's part of being human. The reason that we are sometimes not in control of our actions is that what we do is influenced by many factors. The way in which we were raised, our education, and our present environment all influence what we do. In this respect, your actions are really a result of *you* plus *everyone you've ever known* plus *everything you've ever experienced*. This point of view shifts responsibility away from you. If you are not wholly in control of your actions, then you are not wholly responsible for the outcome, and you should not carry all of the guilt associated with that outcome.

If you feel bad about something that you did in the past, this means that whatever action you feel bad about is not consistent with your current values. If the action is not consistent with your values at the time, then it is clear that you were not in control of the action. If the action *was* in line with your values *at the time*, but your values have changed, then you should not feel bad about that action because you were living authentically at the time. You are a different person now, and the best you can do is to love authentically in the present.

When you are worrying or dwelling, you are preventing yourself from any action. Think about it this way. **You can either dwell or act.** Both require thought, but one is productive while the other is not. The former will keep you guilt-tripping in your present while the latter is the start to changing your present. You are not defined by this situation. You are not who you are at this moment, you have the ability to change. Sometimes we feel ashamed at the thought of changing so drastically—we think: "I was so [insert negative adjective] in that situation that it would seem totally fake if I tried to fix the situation," or, "I deserve this pain." But you are not defined by the situation. You can make the decision to extinguish negative thoughts so you have room for positive action. Or anything else—just remember that occupying your mind with certain thoughts means you have no space for *anything else*... Think this way, is this what you want to be stuck with?

Chapter 3: Developing Empathy for Yourself

A major roadblock to forgiving yourself is the habit of equating your actions to your self-worth. When we do something that we consider to be "bad", we tend to think that means that we are bad *as human beings*. This is an association that we get as children from our parents. When we made mistakes as children, our parents were likely to reprimand us by saying something like "Bad Kate!" Conversely, if a child does something correctly, instead of being praised for completing a task or doing a job well, she is told she is a "good girl". These days, psychologists and parenting experts warn parents to steer clear of these kinds of phrases. This is because as children, we are not emotionally aware enough to understand that the parent is really saying that the *action* is bad, not that we are bad *as people*. When we learn this as children, we continue to equate our actions to our self-worth in adulthood.

In this situation, it may be helpful to view yourself in the past as a different person—a previous version of yourself. That person did not have the experiences that you have had. That person is ignorant of things that you are knowledgeable about. So why would you expect that person - the previous version of you - to make the same decisions and take the same actions that the you today (who has more experience and knowledge) would make and take? **This is an important step in empathizing with yourself.** Take yourself back to when you performed the action. Given the same circumstances, awareness, perspective, needs, desires, and knowledge, would you have done things differently? Or would you have done the exact same thing? If you're honest with yourself, you will find that you truly did the best you could have done back in that moment.

Let's look at the flipside of this scenario. What if you find that the past version of yourself, the one that faltered so badly causing all this guilt, truly did not choose the best course of action at that time? It was clear that you could have done better—not made a rash decision, not given in to temptation, tried harder—and you just *didn't*. It is not necessarily something you can explain. How do you deal with this? Haunting guilt is often the result of being regretful about your actions in the past because you cannot reconcile your actions with your view of yourself. You either are not able to justify your actions, or you have brought your personal identity and understanding of self into question. Here, it is crucial to look *beyond yourself* and **empathize with others** in the situation.

If you are spending all your energies on yourself—your thoughts, your guilt, your situation, your relationships with others—you may be neglecting others in the situation that may have been hurt or compromised. It is wise to take some time and put yourself in their shoes. Think about their perspective—how central are you to their problems? Could they benefit from an apology or a kind gesture? It always helps to think in terms of the Golden Rule. How would you like to be treated if you were in their shoes? Empathizing with others thus helps in two ways. First, it gives you perspective on what others are going through. If you continue to think about how you can play a part in making them feel better, it will also make you feel good and help you in forgiving yourself. Second, it pulls you away from thinking about yourself. You may find that you may have been dwelling on your own situation for far too long, and in this new light it becomes easier to forgive yourself.

Chapter 4: Considering Life as a Classroom

It is important to realize that **we learn by making mistakes**. If you never made a mistake, then you would never learn the difference between "right" and "wrong". If you can view life as a classroom, then it will be easier for you to forgive yourself. After all, would you treat a child the way you are treating yourself? Would you continually scold and berate them for past mistakes? Or would you be more understanding because they are, after all, still learning. Well, the truth is that we are all like children in life— we are all constantly learning. You will always be more aware today than you were yesterday. Just as it is not fair to judge a child from the perspective of an adult, it is not fair to judge yesterday's version of you with the awareness that you have today.

Sometimes you may struggle to forgive yourself because you feel that you knew better and you did a "bad" thing anyway. This line of thinking is due to opposing needs. You may have a long-term desire, such as saving money. However, you may also have a short term desire, like buying a new pair of shoes. These two desires are opposing. If you buy the shoes, you may feel later that it was a mistake because you should have saved the money. But that is only because now, having purchased the shoes, you have a broader perspective on the matter. Now you have the experience of purchasing the shoes, and you can judge the situation with **more knowledge**. You bought the shoes because you thought it was the best decision at the time. Otherwise, you wouldn't have done it! It's also important to remember that, in this saving vs. buying shoes example scenario, you do not have the experience of *not* buying the shoes. It is possible that you would have regretted the decision to forgo the purchase just as much.

Finally, in learning from the past it is important to learn to **maintain perspective**. Was a car ruined? Is your reputation stained? Think realistically, these are not nearly as important as the fact that you are sitting here healthy enough to read and process these words. Material objects and social problems are nowhere as valuable as the life that you have and what you do with it.

Finding value in your mistakes makes it easier for you to forgive yourself. Having made mistakes, you are now able to clearly see a bigger picture (including the consequences of these mistakes) which you can use to be a better person now and in the future. There is an opportunity to learn from almost anything. If you can reframe your situation to see it as an opportunity to grow, you will be rewarded. You will be able to forgive yourself by understanding that internalizing lessons now will lead to a better *you* in the future. Integrity is important here—stick to your commitments to change so you do not find yourself in a similar situation again.

Chapter 5: Learning to Evolve

The most crucial lesson to learn if you want to forgive yourself is that guilt is **not productive**. If you feel bad about something, it is because you wish you could go back and make things right or do things better. But you can't go back. The past is the past; we do not have any control over it. We need to let go of these thoughts.

To learn this we have to stop equating our actions with our identity. We think that since we have done something bad, we are bad as human beings. Again, these thoughts are both incorrect and unhelpful. Remember, the belief that a person is "bad" is partly due to our conditioning growing up. In the previous chapters, we touched on how our elders said "So and so is a bad boy for having done a bad thing," (even when the "bad" thing was merely the accidental a broken glass that slipped from a small boy's hand). Understanding that your worth or value is not dictated by your past mistakes frees you to do better now and in the future.

Ask yourself: **what was the narrative** surrounding the "bad" thing you did in the past? What story were you telling yourself when you performed the action?

What assumptions did you have? Was the story accurate? Were your assumptions true? If not, then get the story straight! Discover what thoughts or ways of thinking lead you to make the mistake. Then, change your ways of thinking.

If possible, it is helpful to **make amends** for whatever action you feel guilty about. Identify others involved and speak to them. See what their concerns are, understand their situation. You will find ways to make amends, as well as find new perspectives from which to view the situation. We often have difficulty forgiving ourselves because we can only see the problem from one angle, and when talking to others we realize the stories they are telling themselves. We feel less isolated and less stuck in our own stories. Such situations can even help you **evolve your communication skills**, since you might be put in the uncomfortable or trying situation of being candid yet sympathetic with others. Take the opportunity to confidently express yourself in your own style of communication. Even if you want to speak from a place of guilt or anger, choose your words wisely and do not simply use them to hurt others. Use your words productively, and **speak your truth**.

To know your truth, you need to know yourself. A way to evolve through such predicaments is by **confronting yourself and your fears.** This is an additional important benefit that can arise from learning to forgive oneself. Progress and changes in life only become possible when we understand ourselves well enough to know why we cannot move past something.

Finally, do what you can **in the present** to be true to the person that you are now. Do not let your past actions limit the extent to which you change for the better. It will take a lot of effort to catch and remind yourself of this new perspective, but it will always benefit you and those around you. Ultimately you will feel lighter and more peaceful as a result of living more in the present.

Conclusion

What we discussed here all essentially lead to the same thing. That is, guilt and related negative emotions are stagnant. These take us nowhere and are unproductive. But you don't need to be ruled by guilt and what has passed. You have the capacity to take proactive action and focus on what matters. Do not waste any more time fretting over what has already happened. It is time to reflect more realistically on what you need to forgive yourself for. And *why* you need to forgive yourself. It should be an organic, concerted effort originating from your own thoughts. If it comes from within, you will truly be able to forgive yourself. Understand that each mistake served a purpose as a learning experience and it will make you a better person.

Someday, you and everyone you know will be gone. That someday is sooner than you think. It is important to live life to the fullest and part of this is through expressing your emotions before they become caught up inside you and grow out of proportion. Normalize these negative emotions. Acknowledge that guilt is a completely natural emotion, and know that it is harmful if left unchecked. Share this with those you love who also have to deal with them at one point or another—dealing with such emotions and learning how to forgive is a crucial part of personal growth. If you learn this now, you are taking the steps needed to becoming a stronger and more capable person. Start the journey to forgiveness today.

Finally, I'd like to thank you for purchasing this book! If you found it helpful, I'd greatly appreciate it if you'd take a moment to leave a review on Amazon. Thank you!

Made in the USA
Lexington, KY
26 September 2019